IN THE
Breaking
OF THE BREAD

52 MEDITATIONS *on the*
MEAL *of* REMEMBRANCE

J. LEE MAGNESS

Standard®
P U B L I S H I N G
Bringing The Word to Life

Cincinnati, Ohio

Published by Standard Publishing, Cincinnati, Ohio
www.standardpub.com
Copyright © 2007 by Lee Magness

Interior design: Edward Willis Group, Inc.

07 08 09 10 11 12   9 8 7 6 5 4 3 2 1

TABLE OF CONTENTS

A CRACK IN THE CUP

> For I received from the Lord what I also passed on to you:
> The Lord Jesus, on the night he was betrayed, took bread,
> and when he had given thanks, he broke it and said,
> "This is my body, which is for you; do this
> in remembrance of me." (1 Corinthians 11:23,24)

There's a crack in the pulpit of the old country church. The front panel of the pulpit where the Gospel is preached every Lord's day has a crack running from top to bottom. At first glance you wish someone would fix it—glue it, clamp it, plastic-wood it, replace it.

But the more you look at it, the more you learn from it. The more you live with it, the more it becomes a reminder that each of us is cracked, marred by sin. It helps us recall, in one way or another, the brokenness with which we approach God and in which he approaches us.

Then one day another crack appeared—a cracked cup, a V-shaped chip out of the lip of a small glass Communion cup. Should it be kept or discarded? What if the cup cut someone's lip? Their blood mingled with the Messiah's. The cup was kept and became a reminder that each of us is cracked, marred by sin.

For some of us the cracks are superficial, for others they are deep, heart-deep. For some of us the cracks are recent, for others they have haunted us for years, growing ever longer, ever wider, ever deeper. Some of us are painfully aware of our cracks, while others have grown comfortable with our cracks, oblivious to what is obvious to others.

But that is why we are here, on this day, and at this table. That is precisely why we eat and why we drink. Not to celebrate our brokenness, but to remember it, and by remembering it to remember him, who was broken on our broken behalf.

God, believing that you came to us and among us in our brokenness, we thank you for saving us from the consequences of our brokenness, for forgiving us in and of our brokenness, through Jesus, Amen.

There's a crossword puzzle in the Gospels. It's a puzzle in the words that Jesus spoke from the cross in the Gospels.

Clue #1: At the moment of his death he was talking about the life of others: "Father, forgive them, for they know not what they do."

Clue #2: At the moment of his rejection as a rebel he was talking about the repentance of a revolutionary: "Today you will be with me in paradise."

Clue #3: At the decisive moment of the dispensation of the ages he was talking about the disposition of his aging mother: "Woman, behold your son; Behold your mother."

Clue #4: At the moment of personal defeat he was talking about spiritual triumph: "It is accomplished."

Clue #5: At the moment of his greatest personal tragedy he was talking about his great personal trust: "Father, into your hands I commend my spirit."

There's a crossword puzzle in the Gospels that has to do with Jesus' puzzling words from the cross. But there is also a crossword puzzle in this meal. There's a puzzle in the words that we speak when we gather for this memorial of the cross.

Clue #1: We celebrate life in him while we talk about his death: "This is my body broken for you."

Clue #2: We remember and repent of the sin which broke our relationship with God while we talk of our reconciliation with God: "This cup is the new covenant in his blood."

It's a crossword puzzle all of whose answers are found right here: "For all have sinned and fall short of the glory of God, and are justified by his grace, through the redemption that came by Christ Jesus." Glory, God, grace, gift, redemption, Christ—may these crosswords, these words of the cross, guide us ever crosswards.

God, we thank you for filling in the blanks of our empty lives, for solving the puzzle of our sin, for saving the puzzled and turning us crosswards, through Jesus, Amen.

The letter of Jude warns disciples of the dangers of false teachers, who were somehow undermining even their Communion at the Lord's table. In the midst of that warning we learn that early Christians called their celebrations of the Lord's Supper "love feasts." They appear to have served a full meal, a carry-in dinner, concluding with and climaxed by the Lord's Supper. Whatever the menu, however lavish the larder, they called it a love feast. In fact in the Greek text there is no word for "feast." Jude refers to the meals simply as "your loves."

What makes this ancient term so appropriate and why don't we use it today? Perhaps it reminds us too much of ancient orgies or modern love-ins. Whatever the reason, love-feast is a concept worth continuing.

The Lord's Supper celebrates a love we cannot *earn*. Jesus' sacrifice is a gift, a gift that flows from God's grace, not our own goodness. And the Lord's Supper celebrates a love we cannot *learn*. God's love in Christ must be experienced and lived out, performed in the practicing.

On the other hand, the Lord's Supper celebrates a love that we must *discern*. The object of love must recognize its source. We must discern his body, the body of Christ, broken for us. And the Lord's Supper celebrates a love we must *return*. Christian love is mutual, reciprocal. We love God because he first loved us. And we love others because we were once the "other" that God loved through Christ.

The Lord's Supper is truly a feast of love. So today let us celebrate God's love, a love we can neither earn nor merely learn. Let us celebrate God's love, discerning the source of his love and returning his love. Today, when we eat and drink, let's have a love feast, a no-holds-barred, anything-goes love feast. Eat, drink, and love one another!

God, whatever else we come to your table to do— commune with you in Communion, eat with you at the Lord's Supper, give thanks to you at the Eucharist—help us always to celebrate your love at this love feast, through Jesus, Amen.

A HOLY MEAL, A HUMAN MEAL

By this time it was late in the day, so his disciples came to him. "This is a remote place," they said, "and it's already very late. Send the people away so they can go to the surrounding countryside and villages and buy themselves something to eat." But he answered, "You give them something to eat." . . . Taking the five loaves and the two fish and looking up to heaven, he gave thanks and broke the loaves. Then he gave them to his disciples to set before the people. (Mark 6:35-37,41)

The words were simple, the actions mundane: he took, he blessed, he broke, he poured, he spoke, he gave. But on Jesus' lips the words became profound, and at Jesus' fingertips the actions became sacred, humans participating in the holy. We call it the Last Supper.

The words, no matter how often repeated, are still simple. The actions, no matter how often reenacted, are still mundane. We take, we bless, we break, we pour, we speak, we give. But spoken in the name of Jesus even our words become profound, and done in the name of Jesus even our actions become sacred, humans participating in the holy. We call it the Lord's Supper.

But this supper reminds us of an even earlier supper, and that earlier supper teaches us something about this supper. The words were simple, the actions mundane: he had them sit down on the grass, he took bread and fish, he gave thanks, he gave it to the disciples, and they gave it to the crowd. "You give them something to eat."

The words are still simple, the actions still mundane: we see the hungry, physically and spiritually, we take what we possess in abundance, we give thanks, we divide it, we give it to those who hunger or who will give it to those who hunger.

And that act—that act of generosity, spoken and done in the name of Jesus— becomes both profound and sacred, humans participating in the holy. You give them something to eat.

God, may this holy meal that you have given us become our model for feeding others in your holy name, through Jesus, Amen.

But when the time had fully come, God sent his Son, born of a woman, born under law, to redeem those under law, that we might receive the full rights of sons. (Galatians 4:4,5)

The scene is a sparse hill in ancient Judea, not far from Jerusalem. Nearby is a cave. Jesus wears one meager garment. Mary watches, wondering what it all means. A man stands by, not the father of Jesus, but the one who will care for her. Beneath Jesus are beams of rough wood. Above, the heavens sparkle with supernatural splendor. In the city sits Herod, pondering Jesus' death. Jewish leaders discuss his coming. Nearby are outcasts, giving their own crude testimony. Soon the rich arrive with gifts, better for burial than for birth.

What did you picture? A birth or a death? A crèche or a cross?

The hill could be a sheep-studded hill near Bethlehem, or the hill called Golgotha. The cave could be a stable crudely cut into one of Bethlehem's hills or a burial vault recently carved in a nearby cemetery. The garment could be swaddling clothes or a bloody, ragged loincloth.

It is Jesus of course, but is he a newborn baby or a dying man? And it is Mary, but is she sitting at a cradle comforting her baby or crouching, crying, herself in need of comfort? Is the man Joseph the carpenter, or John, who will make her a home? Are the wooden beams a manger or a cross? Are they eyeing a cold, clear star or an eclipsed sun and a blood-red moon?

The Herod could be "the Great" who tried to kill the baby or his son who in a sense succeeded. The outcasts could be shepherds, kneeling on either side, or subversives, hanging on either side. The rich men could be magi who offer exorbitant gifts or Nicodemus and Joseph who offer only an empty tomb.

There's a mirror in the manger, a birth reflecting a death. So there is no better way to celebrate Christmas than to keep Communion.

God, thank you for sending your Son, to be born, to live, to die, and to live again. We celebrate him this day and pray in his name, Amen.

Therefore, I urge you, brothers, in view of God's mercy, to offer your bodies as living sacrifices, holy and pleasing to God—which is your spiritual worship. Do not conform any longer to the pattern of this world, but be transformed by the renewing of your mind. Then you will be able to test and approve what God's will is— his good, pleasing and perfect will. (Romans 12:1,2)

The powerful World War I novel, *All Quiet on the Western Front*, became a popular motion picture in 1933. The lead role was won by an up-and-coming actor named Lew Ayres. Many people around the world have read the novel, many more have seen the film, and a few may even remember the promising young actor.

But most people do not know that the experience of acting out the horrors of that war transformed Lew Ayres. He became convinced that he could not with a clear conscience kill another, even in warfare. So, when World War II broke out, he filed for and received conscientious objector status and promptly volunteered to serve as a chaplain and medic on the European front. In spite of his sacrificial service, Ayres' decision ruined his movie career. When the war was over, no one would take a risk on this noncombatant whose role in a movie had become real in his life.

We too have been cast in a drama about a great battle between the forces of sin and death and salvation and life, the re-enactment of the death of Jesus. When we break this bread and share this cup, we act out his death until he comes again.

But will playing this role become real for us? Will re-enacting his death transform our lives? Will it make us new people, with new priorities? Will we find ourselves not only playing our part in the drama of this meal, the drama of salvation, but living out the life-affirming principles of our Lord in the face of the death-dealing principles of our age? And if our conscience answers, Yes, are we willing to face the consequences?

God, we pray, whenever we eat this meal and re-enact his death, that it always be for us more than play-acting, through Jesus, Amen.

A SECOND COMING

So Joseph also went up from the town of Nazareth in
Galilee to Judea, to Bethlehem the town of David. . . . He
went there to register with Mary, who was pledged to be
married to him and was expecting a child. (Luke 2:4,5)

As the time approached for him to be taken up . . .
Jesus resolutely set out for Jerusalem. (Luke 9:51)

They journeyed to Judea—Joseph closing his shop,
Mary pregnant, too pregnant for such a taxing trip. To
Bethlehem, with its sheep and shepherds, soldiers and
shopkeepers, all ready to fleece them. They borrowed a
stall from a friendly farmer. Maybe Mary rode a donkey
or maybe she felt each jarring step. Folk from the fields
celebrated his arrival—shepherds shaken by the shouts
of "Glory to God in the highest," praising God for the child
that had come at last, at long last, Mary agreed. Powerful
people asked, "Who is this?"—magistrates and magi,
scholars and scribes, wondering who and where and when.
It was the first advent, the first coming—soon Jesus would
be born.

They journeyed to Judea—the Son with his face set,
the disciples dragging behind. To Bethany, a farming
village full of friends, followers who would give him shelter.
Jesus rode a donkey— on a journey as long as it was short,

but all dust and tears. Folk from the fields celebrated his arrival—bringing branches, shouting, "Blessed be God," laying down the leafy limbs, hoisting their Hosannas. He had come at last, at long last, they agreed. Powerful people asked, "Who is this?"—rulers and revolutionaries, scholars and scribes, wondering who and what and why. It was the second advent, the second coming. Soon Jesus would die.

Why would we keep Communion at Christmas? Why remember his death at the time of his birth? Why think about the journey at the end of his life while we celebrate the one at the beginning? Because the first journey reminds us of the pain that would return at the end. And the second journey reminds us of the purpose that was present from the very beginning.

God, help us to remember all Jesus' triumphal entries, not the least of which is into our lives, through Jesus, Amen.

ALL OF US

Is not the cup of thanksgiving for which we give thanks a participation in the blood of Christ? And is not the bread that we break a participation in the body of Christ? Because there is one loaf, we, who are many, are one body, for we all partake of the one loaf. (1 Corinthians 10:16,17)

This is not just a pageant, this breaking of the bread, this out-pouring of the cup. It is a feast for us to participate in—all of us. This is not a concert or a lecture or a demonstration, not something done to us or for us. It is something done by us—all of us.

If it is in any sense a drama, it is a drama in which we are not the on-lookers, not the applauders. We are not the audience but the actors—all of us. And our play has its props, but they number only three. There is the loaf—his body broken for us—all of us. And there is the cup—the cup of the new covenant in his blood poured out for us—all of us. But there is also the table, not an altar for priests and presbyters, not a stage for the star alone, but a table, reminding us that we are the guests, that we have our part to play in the play—all of us.

And who is this all-of-us who have come to this table? We are migrant workers and business executives and shopkeepers. We are unemployed. We are children, elderly, single, married. We went through grade school, we have a

Ph.D. We are rich, and . . . not rich. And we have all-of-us come to this table because someone invited us and died for us and rose for us and lives for us. But aren't we sinners? Yes, all of us. The same all-of-us sinners he saved.

The one who gave us himself has given us parts in his great drama of redemption. We are not the audience, we are the actors—all of us.

God, thank you for inviting us to share the loaf and the cup, and thank you for inviting us to sit around the table, together, all of us, through Jesus, Amen.

AMELIA EARHART LUGGAGE

When you come together, it is not the Lord's Supper you eat, for as you eat, each of you goes ahead without waiting for anybody else. One remains hungry, another gets drunk. (1 Corinthians 11:20)

What if you opened one of the catalogs that inundates your mailbox and you happened upon a page offering Amelia Earhart Luggage for sale? Or what if you saw it in one of those glossy magazines that are more advertisement than information or during one of those more-commercial-than-content television programs? Amelia Earhart Luggage!

Who would want to buy luggage named for a world traveler whose plane crashed somewhere in the Pacific? Imagine the possibilities for advertising slogans. "Buy Amelia Earhart Luggage. The luggage that will never wear out even if you're never found!" "Buy Amelia Earhart Luggage. Looks good in the air and under the water!" "Buy Amelia Earhart Luggage. Won't sink even if you do!"

Somehow I think it just wouldn't sell. It wouldn't sell because there is something inconsistent, something contradictory between the name and the product. It would be like offering a line of O.J. Simpson Designer Gloves or trying to market Richard Nixon Tape Recorders. The name is inconsistent with the product.

What about here at this table? This is the Lord's Supper. He inaugurated it, he infused it with meaning, he instructed us in its use, he commanded its practice, he hosts the gatherings around it, and he qualifies the participants. Most importantly he is present at its commemoration. Is the name consistent with the product?

If we call this the Lord's Supper, we must keep our focus on the Lord—on the elements he chose, on the words he spoke, on the meaning he meant, on the importance he imbued it with.

The Christians of Corinth had turned the Lord's Supper into their supper—about food, about them. Let us resolve to make it about fellowship, about him, about the community of the saved, about the Lord. Let it be said of us, "When you meet together, it *is* the Lord's Supper that you eat."

God, help us remember that this is your table not ours, that we come at your invitation not each others', through Jesus, Amen.

AND EAT WITH YOU

Here I am! I stand at the door and knock. If anyone hears my voice and opens the door, I will come in and eat with him, and he with me. (Revelation 3:20)

Jesus spoke those words, those red-letter words. He is the "I," standing at the door, and more than standing—knocking on the door, and more than knocking—calling through the broad boards of the door. He is the one standing there sad-eyed and thorny-crowned, knocking with raw knuckles cupping a pierced palm, calling as if from the broad beams of the cross, except for the fact that he is standing, standing at the door, knocking.

But on whose door does he knock? To whom does he speak? Not to the lost, but to the found. Not to the loyal, but to the lukewarm, the well-clothed-but-naked, eagle-eyed-but-blind, prosperous-but-pitiful, neither-hot! hot! hot!-nor-chilly-cold, spit-you-out Christians of Laodicea.

And what does he want with them, the lukewarm-like-us Laodicean Christians? What does he want with us? Not just to hear his knock-knock-knocking, not just to open the barred boards of the door, not even just to come in and stand there in awkward, don't-I-remember-you-from-somewhere? silence. He comes to eat with us, to eat with us, and us with him.

These words from the book of Revelation are not about the need for conversion; they are about the need for Communion. They are not about finding Christ for the first time; they are about being found by Christ again and again. They are not so much about salvation-time as about supper-time, supper-with-Jesus time, Lord's-Supper time.

Listen! In the stillness of this moment, listen! He is standing at the door, right now, knocking; and if we can hear his voice in the slurp-gurgle of the juice, and tear open the door as we tear that morsel from the loaf, he will come in to us and eat this meal with us, and us with him.

God, help us to make this meal the open-door policy of our lives, through Christ, Amen.

Take my yoke upon you and learn from me. (Matthew 11:29)

What does that mean—learn from me, or more literally learn *of* me? Whatever it means, it must have something to do with the command that precedes it: "take my yoke upon you." Jesus knew what a yoke was. As a carpenter, he roughed out and planed smooth many a yoke in his day. He knew that no matter how well-formed, how well-fitted, no matter how voluntarily accepted, a yoke is still a burden, a burden to be borne.

Jesus knew what the word "yoke" meant to his fellow rabbis. To them "yoke" referred to the "yoke of the law." Jesus knew what a burden the bearing of the law was. So when he said, "Take *my* yoke upon you," he meant something other than the wooden ones he manufactured as a carpenter, something other than the law he had learned as a boy in synagogue school. He was talking about something that was like a yoke, a burden to be borne, but a bearable burden.

He was talking about the yoke of personal allegiance to him, of humble service to him. And that is what "learn of me" must also ultimately mean—more than learn about my life, more than learn my teachings. It means live my teachings, live my life.

But "take my yoke upon you and learn of me" echoes another saying of Jesus: "Take up my cross and . . . follow me." To take on Christ's yoke is ultimately to take up Christ's cross. To learn of Christ means ultimately to follow Christ.

So when we come to this table, we come to the cross, Christ's cross, but also a cross ready to be borne by us, a yoke of whole-life, life-long allegiance to our Lord. And when we come to this table, we come to a place where we can learn of him, learn the most important facts about him, the saving facts. And when we come to this table, we come to a place where we can, if we dare, follow him—to the cross and beyond.

God, help us to be learners and followers, yoke-fellows and cross-bearers, through the one who bore the cross for us, Amen.

AT THE FOOT OF THE CROSS

> You see, at just the right time, when we were still powerless, Christ died for the ungodly. Very rarely will anyone die for a righteous man, though for a good man someone might possibly dare to die. But God demonstrates his own love for us in this: While we were still sinners, Christ died for us. (Romans 5:6-8)

There they stood at the foot of the cross, standing, not kneeling, priests and scribes, their eyes squinting to slits in the noon-day sun, squinting like the sightless pretending to see. They were blinded by years of looking through glasses tinted with law and tainted by sin. They were blinded by years of looking for the wrong Messiah for the wrong reasons, so set on a sovereign to save them from their servitude that they could not see the Sovereign in the Servant.

There they stood at the foot of the cross, stood, not kneeled, Jewish rulers and Roman soldiers, their every word an irony. They named the criminal, "The King of the Jews," accurate in spite of their spite, inaccurate in the light of his authority over Heaven and earth and them. They threw his words back at his mute mouth, "Aha, the one who would destroy the temple and rebuild it in three days," the feat they thought impossible happening right before their eyes. They called his bluff, saying, "He saved others, let him save himself," not realizing that to really accomplish the one, he could not do the other. Then they said, "Let him come down from the cross, so that we might believe," the final irony, since we believe precisely because he did not . . . come down from the cross.

Here we are gathered around this table, as close to the foot of the cross as we dare to get, care to get, need to get. Standing is hard enough, but we force ourselves to kneel. And we wag our heads in wonder, not that he died, but that he died for such as them, and for such as us, standing, now kneeling, at the foot of the cross.

God, help us to look at the cross with while-we-were-yet-sinners eyes, through Jesus, Amen.

Ignatius, a Christian leader from Antioch, wrote these words in about AD 110 in a letter to the Ephesians:

"A star shone forth in the heaven above all the stars; and its light was unutterable, and its strangeness caused amazement; and all the rest of the constellations with the sun and moon formed themselves into a chorus about the star; but the star itself far outshone them all; and there was perplexity to know whence came this strange appearance which was so unlike them . . . , when God appeared in the likeness of man unto the newness of everlasting life. . . ." (*To the Ephesians,* 19)

More striking than the beauty of these words is the paradox contained in them. Ignatius wrote these words about a birth, the birth of Jesus, and about life, new life, on his way to his death, his martyrdom in Rome. Ignatius wrote these words about the Bethlehem sky full of stars on his way to a Roman arena full of beasts. Ignatius recognized that the strange appearance of the star of stars not only signaled incarnation—God appearing in human likeness—it also signaled eternity—"the newness of everlasting life."

We gather today, commemorating birth and death, celebrating the coming of the incarnate Christ and commemorating the presence of the crucified Christ, all in this one act of worship.

This is his once-baby body, broken for us. And the bread is Word, wondrous Word, become flesh. This is the cup of the new covenant in his blood. And the reflection in the cup is a light around which all the stars gather in amazement—a light that began in Bethlehem but culminated at Calvary.

When we partake, we do so in celebration of his birth, in remembrance of his death, and in anticipation of life, everlasting life.

God, we take these tokens of his death as a token of his birth and as a token of our life, through Jesus, Amen.

CARRYING THE WOOD

> Abraham took the wood for the burnt offering and placed
> it on his son Isaac, and he himself carried the fire and the
> knife. As the two of them went on together, Isaac spoke up
> and said to his father Abraham, "Father?" "Yes, my son?"
> Abraham replied. "The fire and wood are here,"
> Isaac said, "but where is the lamb for the burnt offering?"
> Abraham answered, "God himself will provide the lamb
> for the burnt offering, my son." (Genesis 22:6-8)

They were both sons, both beloved sons, both only sons, both children of promise on whom the father's future depended. A son named Laughter, now come to mourning. A son named Salvation, about to lose his life.

They were both directed to a mountain, along a path paved with sorrows, with two companions at their sides. They were directed by the will of the father. And yet they were adult sons, both in their early 30's, sons whose wills had to cooperate with their fathers' wills if their fathers' wills were to be carried out.

They both bore the branches. Both had to carry the very wood they would be sacrificed on. Both wondered where the lamb was.

And finally figuring out fully where their path led, they both said, "Father." One father replied for the other, "God himself will provide the lamb for a burnt offering, my son."

There the stories diverge. Laughter was not sacrificed, rather a ram caught in the thicket. Salvation died, a lamb caught in the thorns. In the deliverance of the one son we learn that God will provide. In the death of the other, the one and only, we learn that...God will provide.

When we come to this table, we come more like Laughter than Salvation. We come trusting that God will not only provide, but that he is right here with us. We come of our own accord, but also in response to the tug of God's grace. We come carrying the kindling, the instrument of our own immolation, our sin. But it is the lamb-Son of God who carried the wood, under and on its dark beams, in our place.

God, help us to follow the one who carried the wood, through Jesus, Amen.

CHRIST IS ALL IN ALL

Christ is all, and is in all. (Colossians 3:11)

Who is our host, this Christ we come to commune with? What do we make of this body we discern and this blood we drink? Who is this man, the motive for our meal?

He is the road and the traveler on the road. He is the guide for travelers on the road and the destination at the end of the road. He is the host who welcomes us home when we reach the end of the road.

He is the root and the shoot from which our life springs. He is the trunk from which we branch and bear. He is the blossom, the lily of the valley, in which we delight. He is the fruit that fulfills us and makes us fruitful.

He is the head. He is the hand that helps us. He is the arm that enfolds us. He is the eye that sees in us the us we are. He is the ear that holds us like a shell and hears the cries he cried for us.

Road, root, shoot, fruit. Fruit, vine, fruit of the vine. Head, hand, eye, ear. Who is this Christ who consumes all our categories, who infiltrates every area of our lives? This one who is our all in all is also all in all at this table.

He is the Host who invites us to the feast, the Servant who washes our feet, the Guest ever present. He is the Bread we eat, the Cup we drink. We come at his call, not at our own inclination. We pause at the door to let him, our Savior-Servant, wash our feet, though we should be washing his. We scoot over to make room for the Guest who has made room for us, knowing we don't deserve a place and that's why we're here. We eat the bread, though it was broken because of our brokenness. We accept the cup he didn't refuse, although he did not deserve it.

Christ is all and in all, all the reason we need to share this meal.

God, we pray that Christ be all things in all ways to us all, Amen.

> Though they found no proper ground for a death
> sentence, they asked Pilate to have him executed.
> When they had carried out all that was written
> about him, they took him down from the tree
> and laid him in a tomb. (Acts 13:28,29)

Your Christmas tree may be fir-green or pine-green or spruce-green, but it is green, green as life. Even if it is synthetic, it is probably green, green like life. And the ornaments, balls or bulbs, bangles or beads, probably glitter, glitter like light.

But that beautiful tree is only a pale shadow of the original Christmas tree. It was a stunningly stark tree, dark, bare of balls or bulbs. But you can't understand or celebrate or even have Christmas without that tree.

If we could decorate that tree, we would want to place a bright and morning star at its top, to remind us that Jesus is the light of the world. We would adorn it with golden crowns, to remind us that Jesus is the King of the Jews. We would add scarlet bows, to remind us that Jesus was born of woman.

We might wind white ribbon 'round its tall trunk, to remind us that Jesus is son of Mary, son of David, son of Abraham, son of Adam. And we would keep, not cut, its great roots, to remind us that Jesus is the Son of God. That's what we would do if we could have decorated the first Christmas tree.

But the original Christmas tree had only one gruesome garland, a bloody body, draped limply over its limbs. And it had but one ugly ornament, a splintered sign carrying but one sentence, Jesus of Nazareth, King of the Jews.

It is that Christmas tree, gaunt not green, bloody not bright, that we set up on this table around which we gather. It is of course a cross, not gold or bejeweled, but planed wood and plain. Is there nothing that we can add, no adornment we can contribute to its beauty? Only this: we may adorn it with our lives.

God, help us see with new eyes, eyes energized by this bread and cup, true light emanating from the true tree. We pray through Jesus, Amen.

COLD BREAD AND WARM WINE

When he was at the table with them, he took the bread,
gave thanks, broke it and began to give it to them.
And their eyes were opened and they recognized him,
and he disappeared from their sight. They asked each
other, "Were not our hearts burning within us while
he talked with us on the road and opened the scriptures
to us?" They got up and returned at once to Jerusalem.

(Luke 24:30-33)

"They got up and returned at once to Jerusalem." This
is just one of the wonderful statements in Luke's account of
the appearance of the risen Lord to the two people on the
road to Emmaus.

What's wonderful about it is that these two have been
worrying all weekend about how their Christ had turned
to a corpse. They have been wearying their way to their
walk's end, seven dreary miles home. Then they barely sit
down for a bleary-eyed meal with a suspicious stranger,
when he becomes a sight for soar-eyes, and he is gone
from their sight, and they are jumping up from the table,
wending their dusky way back to the future.

Why the sudden return?

The resurrection of Jesus is like that. It has that kind
of impact. It made them leave the warm, flat bread on the
table to cool and go hard. It made them leave the cold, full-

bodied wine on the table to warm and go flat. It made them get up and go all the seven miles back to the Jerusalem they had just come seven miles from. It made them set out in the dark that was darker than the dark that had been too dark for Jesus to go on.

It is at this table that we recognize Jesus and the reality of the resurrection. It is this table that makes us get up and return at once to whatever daily life we have dragged ourselves from, and say, the Lord is risen!

God, thank you for asking us to come and sit at a meal that makes us so able, so eager, to jump up from it with joy. Help us to live in the reality of the resurrection, through Jesus, Amen.

COMMUNION AND COMMUNITY

They devoted themselves to the apostles' teaching and to the fellowship, to the breaking of bread and to prayer. . . . Every day they continued to meet together in the temple courts. They broke bread in their homes and ate together with glad and sincere hearts. (Acts 2:42,46)

They devoted themselves to the breaking of bread. And day by day they broke bread in their homes. Unless Luke, the author of the book of Acts, is being uncharacteristically redundant, he is reporting on two important and intertwined activities pursued by the earliest Christians. His first reference seems to be what we call Communion, the Lord's Supper—the breaking of the bread. The second appears to be a reference to community meals—breaking bread. If so, they took both activities very seriously, Communion and community.

And why not? These two characteristics of the Christian life cannot exist without the other. Communion must take place in the community of believers. It was never meant to be a solitary thing, a microwave meal for one eaten in isolation from others. And community, Christian community, must always be centered on Communion. The fellowship of the saints would not even exist if God in Christ had not transformed us through the very event this meal commemorates.

The earliest Christians took both Communion and community very seriously. And so must we.

We fellowship not only with the Host, the Savior, but also with the other guests, the saved. We celebrate the death of his body on the cross, and we celebrate the life of his body, the church. Whenever we gather, even two or three of us, we gather in his name, knowing that the crucified and risen Lord is in our midst. Whenever we remember his death, we do so conscious that his blood was poured out for the person next to us as surely as for us.

Let us devote ourselves to the breaking of the bread. But let us also break bread in our homes, with glad and generous hearts.

God, help us to enrich our Communion by a consciousness of our community, and help us to enrich our community by our consciousness of Communion, through Jesus, Amen.

Reenactments are all the rage. People gather to reenact historical events of regional or national significance—events that have made us who we are or brought us to the place we now find ourselves. It may be the arrival of a great leader like a Lincoln. It may be a mass movement of many people like the March on Washington or the Trail of Tears. Often it's a decisive battle that turned the tide of a war. For one day or one weekend, we dress up and eat and sleep and talk, we live like, say, Washington's troops at Valley Forge. We remember what someone did by doing it, not precisely perhaps, but close enough to be reminded of it in and by the re-doing.

What we do here today is a reenactment, reenacting an event that made us what we are and brought us to the place we find ourselves. It involved the action of a great leader, our Savior, and it connects us to the mass movement of a great people, the body of Christ. And it is the reenactment of an on-going battle in a war that has already been won. This Lord's Supper reminds us of the Last Supper, and the bread and cup remind us of the symbols he shared, symbols of life and death. We even recite the very words of the very one whose acts we reenact.

Do this, Jesus said, in remembrance of me. So we *re*member by re-doing, reenacting the events that made us who we are—saved—and brought us to the place we find ourselves—sanctified.

God, help us in our reenactment to remember not only the act but also the one who acted on our behalf, through Jesus, Amen.

ENTRY AND EXIT

> He sent two of his disciples, saying to them, "Go to the village ahead of you, and as you enter it, you will find a colt tied there, which no one has ever ridden. Untie it and bring it here. . . ." Those who were sent ahead went and found it just as he had told them. (Luke 19:29,30,32)
>
> Jesus sent Peter and John, saying, "Go and make preparations for us to eat the Passover. . . ." He replied, "As you enter the city, a man carrying a jar of water will meet you. Follow him to the house that he enters. . . ." They left and found things just as Jesus had told them. (Luke 22:8,10,13)

Two different events in Jesus' life have something in common—they are the most carefully planned, most meticulously orchestrated events of his whole ministry. They are the Triumphal Entry and the Last Supper.

The Triumphal Entry wound down dusty paths outside the city. It was not for the priests who had everything pinned-down and pigeon-holed, but the pilgrims, the eager, expectant, early-morning pilgrims who clogged those dusty-dawn-rose roads. And so with the Last Supper, a supper for sinners, for those confused, over-confident betrayers and deniers and doubters whom he invited to the table.

The Triumphal Entry was not about prancing stallions

but humble donkeys, not military conquest but spiritual renewal, not power but peace, not throwing off the yoke of servitude but bearing a burden shaped suspiciously like a cross. And so with the Last Supper, a supper that began with Jesus washing his almost washed-up disciples' feet and ended with him calling them beyond sit-at-your-right-hand competition to servant-of-all humility.

The Triumphal Entry ended oddly, in tears, with Jesus weeping over a city teeming with those who wanted redemption without repentance. And so with the Last Supper, a supper where Jesus saw reflected in their eyes arrogance and fear and confusion and betrayal—and decided to die for it.

Today we celebrate a triumph acted out ultimately not on a donkey on the Mount of Olives but on a cross on Golgotha. Do this in remembrance of him.

God, forgive us for being more like those disciples than we care to be. And thank you for being as forgiving as ever, through Jesus, Amen.

FAMILIARITY BREEDS . . .

When he was at the table with them, he took bread, gave thanks, broke it and began to give it to them. Then their eyes were opened and they recognized him. (Luke 24:30,31)

Why is it that so often, when Jesus appeared to his followers after the resurrection, he was eating? First in Jerusalem, then in Galilee, now in Emmaus, why was he always eating?

It may be because we see each other, the real each other, best at mealtime, at the point of our common need, in the midst of a common act.

And why is it that be-our-guest Jesus suddenly became the host in Emmaus? If he had been invited by someone else to someone else's house to eat someone else's food at someone else's table, why was he acting like the host?

It may be that Jesus had a way of becoming the host even when he was the guest, preferring to serve than to be served.

And why is it that they recognized him when they did? Not as companion or questioner or teacher but as bread-breaker? Why then and why that?

Some think they saw for the first time the strange scars on his bread-breaking hands. But others think they saw something not strange at all but familiar, the familiar hands going through the familiar motions. Had they seen him break bread for the five thousand, for the four thousand, for the twelve in the Upper Room?

We've all done this before, this breaking of the bread, this taking of the cup. Every Sunday for every year for who knows how many years, we've done this over and over. Some might say that such familiarity might breed a kind of contempt.

But that is simply not the case, at least in this case. A familiar setting, a meal. A familiar role for Jesus, serving. A familiar act, breaking the bread, drinking the cup. Familiarity breeds . . . recognition. He is known to us in the breaking of the bread.

God, we pray that our holy habit might continue to make this meal more not less. We pray not for repetition but for recognition, through Jesus, Amen.

FAST OR FEAST

The kingdom of heaven is like a king who prepared a wedding banquet for his son. (Matthew 22:2)

We may not eat very much when we gather for the Lord's Supper—a fragment of bread and a small cup—but it is a supper, and it is focused on food. What we do here is more like feasting than fasting.

Fasting has its place in the life of Christians. Jesus fasted and recognized the appropriateness of fasting. Fasting is not a way to win the applause of others or the approval of God. It has more to do with our response to God's grace and our recognition of our sin than with God's response to our goodness and his recognition of our sanctity. Fasting does not make us more *acceptable* to God, it makes us more *accessible* to God. But for Jesus the sign of the kingdom was feasting, not fasting.

Jesus himself feasted so frequently that his opponents called him a "glutton" and a "winebibber"! Luke loves to tell mealtime stories of Jesus. Meals were the contexts of some of his most memorable teachings and miracles. He compared his presence to a wedding banquet—a time to eat.

And so when we gather at the Lord's table, commemorating the Lord's presence, we too must celebrate.

It is a Thanksgiving dinner, but better than turkey and stuffing, because this meal reminds us that God has provided not just a harvest but salvation. It is a wedding banquet, but better than cake and punch, because this meal reminds us that we are the bride of Christ, redeemed by him. This is a time for feasting, not fasting.

Some of us here today—many of us, perhaps all of us—have reason to repent, reason to fast. We may have prepared for our worship today by fasting or we may respond by fasting. But for now we eat, we come to the table and eat, eat and rejoice in the salvation it symbolizes. All things are ready, come to the feast.

God, help us to approach this table like people invited to a feast, feasting on the forgiveness that is ours through your Son, our Savior, our Bridegroom. We pray in his name, Amen.

When they landed, they saw a fire of burning coals
there with fish on it, and some bread. Jesus said to them,
"Bring some of the fish you have just caught." Simon Peter
climbed aboard and dragged the net ashore.
It was full of large fish. . . . Jesus said to them,
"Come and have breakfast." (John 21:9-12)

First thing after he first called them, they ate together, a wedding feast at Cana, changing water to wine. Last thing before he died, they ate together, a body-bread, covenant-cup supper in the upper room, changing horror to hope.

First thing after he rose, they ate together, Jesus and the two grief-eyed men of Emmaus, a bread-breaking, eye-opening-at-last meal, changing "We had hoped he was the redeemer" to "We have seen the risen Lord." Last thing before he ascended, they ate together, Jesus and his glory-eyed disciples, Jesus and his you-will-be-my-witnesses disciples, changing fear to faith.

Early in his ministry he ate, ate with thousands of hungry Galileans on the gravelly shore. Later in his ministry he ate again, ate with thousands of hungry Gentiles on the grassy slope.

First thing after the resurrection, Jesus found his disciples gone fishin', fanned the coals into flame, warmed some bread and broiled some fish. Let's have some breakfast, he called, challenging them to exchange one kind of fishing for another. Last thing, after our resurrection, Jesus will eat together with us, a marriage supper of the Lamb.

From first to last, what we do here today, breaking this bread and drinking this cup, has been done in one way or another every yesterday and will be done in one way or another every tomorrow. From first to last, what we do here today, eating and drinking, is the pattern of the past and the occupation of eternity. If Jesus were here today, crouching on the beach of our hopeless harbors, tending the flickering fires of our faith, this is exactly what he would be doing—eating—and he is.

God, we thank you for these artifacts of antiquity, these emblems of eternity, asking that they give us renewed meaning for this moment, through Jesus, Amen.

GO AND LEARN WHAT THIS MEANS

While Jesus was having dinner at Matthew's house, many tax collectors and "sinners" came and ate with him and his disciples. When the Pharisees saw this, they asked his disciples, "Why does your teacher eat with tax collectors and 'sinners'?" On hearing this, Jesus said, "It is not the healthy who need a doctor, but the sick. But go and learn what this means: 'I desire mercy, not sacrifice.' For I have not come to call the righteous, but sinners." (Matthew 9:10-13)

Suppose the kindergarten teacher only admitted five-year-old geniuses into his class. Then most of us would never get an education. Suppose the doctor only agreed to see robustly healthy people in her office. Then most of us would never get well.

Suppose Jesus had come to call only the righteous. Then most of us could never be forgiven by him. Suppose God did require sacrifice for salvation. Then no offering we could ever make would ever remove our offense—we would never be saved.

Suppose the Lord's table was only for those who had neither disappointed nor disobeyed nor doubted their Lord. Then most of us, no, all of us, should pass the bread by unbroken, watch our cupped reflections pass before us undrunk.

Suppose we refused even to gather at the Lord's table, because we judged ourselves guilty. Then we would be truly guilty, not just of sin, not just of unrighteousness, but of refusing to come, to follow, to eat, as sinners, precisely the ones he came to call, precisely the ones for whom he died, precisely the ones for whom this table is spread.

Mercy, what presumption! Not only to reject our relationship with God by sinning, but to reject our reconciliation with God by thinking that this meal is not precisely for us, us sinners. Mercy!

Let us go and learn what this means: This is my body given for you. This is my blood of the covenant, poured out for many for the forgiveness of sins.

God, give us the wisdom and give us the humility, to let you doctor us not just because we are sick, but even though we are sick, through Jesus, Amen.

For whenever you eat this bread and drink this cup,
you proclaim the Lord's death until he comes.
(1 Corinthians 11:26)

Every first Sunday of December the family gathered at
Grandmother's house for her birthday. After more-than-
enough farm food, the relatives settled on the sagging sofas
and over-stuffed chairs to do what relatives do—relate.
Three things always happened.

First, there was a celebration, complete with cake
and candles, well wishes and odd but well-intended gifts
from her grandchildren. Hers was a life worth celebrating.
Second, there was the anticipation of the next time they
would all be together again in just a few over-the-river-and-
through-the-woods weeks—Christmas at Grandmother's
house! It was an event worth anticipating. And third,
the gathering paused for somber recollection. They were
reminded of one time when her birthday fell on a Sunday,
December 7, 1941, Pearl Harbor Day. She rehearsed to her
well-fed family how they had gathered that day as usual,
eaten and relaxed around the radio as usual, only to learn
of something unusual, something unthinkable, an event
that had occurred a world away. It was an event worth
remembering.

At this table we participate in those three activities.

We celebrate Jesus' birth and life and death and rebirth. His was a life—and a death—worth celebrating. And we anticipate the next time we will all be together, not at a birthday party or a Christmas party but a wedding party, the marriage supper of the Lamb. It is an event worth anticipating. And we gather as usual in solemn remembrance of an unusual event, an unthinkable event, not a birthday or a wedding but a death, a world away and an age ago. It is an event worth remembering.

May every Sunday in the life of the extended family we call the church be a time of celebration and anticipation and recollection. May we lean into the past, recalling what Jesus did on the cross, and lean into the future, hoping in what he will do at his return, and may we lift thankful hearts for what he is doing day by day in our lives.

God, help us now to celebrate joyfully, to anticipate hopefully, and to recollect meaningfully, through Jesus, Amen.

HERE AND NOW

But we sailed from Philippi after the Feast of Unleavened Bread, and five days later joined the others at Troas, where we stayed seven days. On the first day of the week we came together to break bread. (Acts 20:6,7)

You've come to the right place. And you've come at the right time.

There is no one for whom here is not the right place, and there is no one for whom now is not the right time. There is no one for whom this table is not the right place, nor for whom what we are about to do here is not the right thing, nor for whom the first day of the week is not the right time.

If we lack understanding, this is where we begin to remember. If we lack fellowship, this is where we begin to become one. If we have sin in our lives (and who doesn't?), this is where we meet mercy. If we have lost our focus, if we feel like we have lost touch, if our lives have become insipid, this is where we begin to see Christ again, touch Christ anew, taste Christ afresh.

You've come to the right place, at the right time, to do the right thing.

This is where Jesus took bread and gave thanks for it, and broke it, and gave it to them, to us, saying, "This is my body, broken for you."

This is when Jesus took the cup, gave thanks for it, poured it out, and shared it with them, with us, saying, "This is the blood of the new covenant, poured out for many."

So just like the Christians of Troas, who came to the right place—together—at the right time—on the first day of the week—to do the right thing—to break bread, so we have come—with the Lord's People, on the Lord's Day, to eat the Lord's Supper.

God, we thank you not only that we are here at the right place and at the right time, but also that you are here, in these elements. And we thank you for Jesus in whom you came in the fullness of time, in his name, Amen.

> When Pilate saw that he was getting nowhere,
> but that instead an uproar was starting, he took
> water and washed his hands in front of the crowd.
> "I am innocent of this man's blood," he said. "It is
> your responsibility!" All the people answered, "Let his
> blood be on us and on our children!" (Matthew 27:24, 25)

Pontius Pilate dishonestly declared, "I am innocent of this man's blood. It is your responsibility!" And then he sent Jesus to his death. But his denial of accountability was no more effective in removing his guilt than a good hand-washing. And his attempt to shift blame onto the crowds was cowardly, if partly true.

The crowds at least answered honestly: "His blood be on us and on our children!" But their acceptance of accountability made their misguided actions no more acceptable.

There is a sense of course in which we all can and should say the same words, the words of the crowd, when we gather at this meal to commemorate his death. We say, "His blood be on us," because we have accepted our guilt, and we have sensed our shame.

But there is another sense in which we all can and should say those same words—but for a completely different reason. We say, "His blood be on us," precisely because we have been "washed in the blood of the Lamb," precisely because he has removed our guilt by the shedding of his blood, and precisely because his sacrifice has freed us from our shame.

When we are tempted to cringe in horror because our sin has caused his death on the cross, let us instead cry out with joy because we are washed in the blood of the Lamb.

And so we say, "His blood be on us," as a way of remembering his sacrifice. We say, "His blood be on us," as a way of repenting of our sin. And we say, "His blood be on us," as a way of rejoicing in his salvation.

God, may his blood be on us and on our children, not just as a result of our sin and guilt, but in recognition of your saving grace, through Jesus, Amen.

IN MEMORY OF HIM, IN MEMORY OF HER

While he was in Bethany, reclining at the table in the home of a man known as Simon the Leper, a woman came with an alabaster jar of very expensive perfume, made of pure nard. She broke the jar and poured the perfume on his head. . . . And they rebuked her harshly. "Leave her alone," said Jesus. "Why are you bothering her? She has done a beautiful thing to me. . . . She did what she could. She poured perfume on my body beforehand to prepare for my burial. I tell you the truth, wherever the gospel is preached throughout the world, what she has done will also be told, in memory of her." (Mark 14:3-9)

In Jerusalem they gathered for a meal, Jesus and his disciples. Jesus took a loaf and shared it with his guests, then the cup and shared it with his guests. Then he told them that whenever they repeated those actions, as often as they ate, to do it in memory of him.

Just a night or two before, in nearby Bethany, they gathered for a meal, a wealthy Pharisee and Jesus and other prominent guests. In slipped a woman who poured expensive ointment on Jesus' head. When the disciples protested, Jesus said, "Wherever the gospel is preached, this will be told in memory of her."

In memory of him, in memory of her.

What did she do that was so special, that deserved to

be remembered, that deserved to share the language of the Lord's Supper, in memory of him, in memory of her?

When others were haughty, she was humble. When others spoke of their appreciation, she acted it out. When others hid under a sin-thin veneer of respectability, she repented, right there in the glare of public opinion.

But ultimately she deserves to be remembered because she remembered him. She would smile through all her pain if she knew that our remembering her makes us remember him.

Today, as we break this bread and share this cup, let us remember him by remembering the her who remembered him.

God, help us live repentantly, in memory of her, and help us live redemptively, in memory of him, through Jesus, Amen.

> "O Jerusalem, Jerusalem, you who kill the prophets and stone those sent to you, how often I have longed to gather your children together, as a hen gathers her chicks under her wings, but you were not willing." (Matthew 23:37)

The Lord's table is the place where we remember best what Jesus did for us. He fed and bled.

First, we break the bread—the bread he broke, the bread he fed them—and hear his words: "Take, eat, this is my body." When they ate the bread, they ate, as it were, his own body, his broken-for-us body. He himself fed them. He fed them himself.

Second, we pour the cup—the cup he willed to drink for us as much as with us—and hear his words, "Drink from it, all of you; for this is my blood of the covenant which is poured out for many for the forgiveness of sins." When they drank from the cup, they drank, as it were, of his very blood, the blood he bled. He *bled* for them. He bled for *them*.

These two actions—this feeding and this bleeding—demonstrate best the self-sacrificial love of a mother. A mother bleeds and feeds. When a mother gives birth, she yields herself to body-wracking, tissue-rending pain. She bleeds us to birth. And when a mother nurses, she yields her very self to sustain us. She feeds us to life.

Just a day or two before the Last Supper, Jesus wished he could, like a mother hen, gather his chicks under his wings. And we are not surprised that Jesus, the one who fed and bled, would want to be as a mother, the one who bleeds and feeds.

But we need to be reminded—like children who have no memory of our own births, who have no recollection of being nursed—that when we gather at this table we eat and drink at the behest of the one who, just like Mommy, once bled for us and feeds us still.

God, help us to remember that in our salvation, you brought us to life, you nurtured us, and you loved us. Help us to gather now as your children, your grateful children, through Jesus, Amen.

"Father, forgive them, for they do not know what they are doing." (Luke 23:34)

Jesus had come to forgive, and he died forgiving. When we gather at this table, we recognize and accept that we are forgiven, and we recognize and accept that if he died forgiving we must live for forgiving.

"Today you will be with me in paradise." (Luke 23:43)

Jesus had come to save, and he died saving. When we gather at this table, we recognize and accept the salvation that has come to us from him. We also celebrate the fact that salvation means being with him wherever and whenever. And we recognize and accept his example and call to be sharers of salvation with all those he died to save.

"Dear woman, here is your son." . . . *"Here is your mother."* (John 19:26, 27)

Jesus had come to create community, and he died forging a new family. When we gather at this table, we recognize and accept our place in a new network of relationships, a new family of faith and fellowship and mutual service.

"My God, my God, why have you forsaken me?" *"I am thirsty."* (Matthew 27:46, John 19:28)

Jesus had come to teach, and he died teaching, quoting messianic prophecies from Psalm 22, pre-minding them of his death until he came again. When we gather at this table, we too teach, showing forth his death until he comes again.

"It is finished." (John 19:30)

Jesus had come with a mission, and he died with his mission on his mind. When we gather at this table, we recognize that we are people with a mission, on a mission, with him and with each other, a mission we are called to complete.

"Father, into your hands I commit my spirit."
(Luke 23:46)

Jesus had come with trust in God, and he died trusting. When we gather at this table, we recognize and accept his death, and we recognize and accept our death, in the light of our trust in the God who gives life.

God, as we gather at this table, help us to forgive the enemy, love the outcast, care for the community, teach the truth, be faithful in ministry, and trust in you, because of Jesus, Amen.

MAKING HISTORY

After Jesus was born in Bethlehem in Judea, during the time of King Herod, Magi from the east came to Jerusalem and asked, "Where is the one who has been born king of the Jews? We saw his star in the east and have come to worship him." (Matthew 2:1,2)

History tends to remember the wrong people or remember the right people for the wrong reasons. History tends to remember the rich and the ruler rather than the righteous and the ragged, unless their rags have turned to riches. It tends to record the powerful rather than the pious or the peaceable.

This was never truer than at the birth of Jesus. Accounts of that time focus on the first emperor, Caesar Augustus—builder of a mighty empire, conqueror of nations. In Judea Herod *the Great* dominates the history books—builder of a kingdom, slaughterer of children, including his own.

But we remember wise men, nameless wise men. Gaspar, Balthasar, and Melchior are later inventions. They were not mighty or majestic. We sing "We Three Kings," but they are never called kings. They were strangers in a strange land, where their wonderful discovery was about to be twisted by the disastrous designs of the "history-maker" Herod. They knew less than the priests and scribes, asking questions rather than providing answers. In fact they are never actually called wise.

But they found Jesus and they worshiped him.

When history remembers today, it will remember politicians and generals and CEOs. It will recall events in Washington or Israel or China.

But this is where it's happening. This table is where His-Story is being made, where nameless strangers in a strange land find and worship Jesus. Where we have come from is not as important as where we have come. Many are poor, most poor in spirit. Few are powerful, all lean on the Lord. What really matters is that "This is his body" and "This cup is the new covenant in his blood." This meal is the most momentous thing that will happen in the world today.

God, help us to make His-Story today, finding him afresh, worshiping him as if all history depended on him. We pray, believing that it does, through Jesus, Amen.

MAKING ROOM FOR JESUS

Then came the day of Unleavened Bread on which the Passover lamb had to be sacrificed. Jesus sent Peter and John, saying, "Go and make preparations for us to eat the Passover." "Where do you want us to prepare for it?" they asked. He replied, "As you enter the city, a man carrying a jar of water will meet you. Follow him to the house that he enters, and say to the owner of the house, 'The Teacher asks: Where is the guest room, where I may eat the Passover with my disciples?' He will show you a large upper room, all furnished. Make preparations there." They left and found things just as Jesus had told them. So they prepared the Passover. (Luke 22:7-13)

Who was that man, masked by our memory, who made room, a guest room, a large upper room, for Jesus? Did he know the Teacher well or at all, or was he only known by him? Was it a servant or a son that he sent to meet the disciples, scratching their heads, eyeing averted eyes, searching the swollen city for who-knows-whom?

Was it a simple fact or a signal, that water-jar, that man carrying a water-jar, against all women-fetch-water convention? Was the water for washing feet, poured and pooled in the bowl still by the door, left to lap at the lip of the basin until the host played household servant?

Why did Jesus call it "my guest room"? Had he roomed

there before, and now made reservations with reservations, leasing it for the least of these his brethren?

And how did it come to be furnished and ready? Did he know—this nameless, faceless man, when he folded the towel, and set the low table, and scattered the cushions—what words of horror and hope would ring out 'round that room, what deeds of service and symbolism would be enacted there?

Do we? Do we know what will come of our done-them-a-thousand-times, do-them-with-our-eyes-closed, more-than-going-through-the-more-than-motions actions, when we, whoever we may be, make room for Jesus?

God, we pray that you help us to make room for Jesus, to make ourselves furnished and ready, for this Communion with him, through Jesus, Amen.

MIRROR, MIRROR

Now we see but a poor reflection as in a mirror; then we shall see face to face. Now I know in part; then I shall know fully, even as I am fully known. (1 Corinthians 13:12)

One Sunday morning he went into the classroom to look for a Bible. There, unexpectedly, he saw his own image, reflected in framed glass hanging on the wall. He paused to involuntarily adjust the knot of his tie. But as he stared, as he studied his own face in the glass, he realized that it was no mirror in which he saw himself. It was Jesus. It was a print of a painting of Jesus he had seen from his youth. Suddenly his straight, graying hair had become brown and wavy. His gray-green, failing eyes had turned deep brown, peering, piercing. His chin had sprouted a full beard.

He saw himself in a new light, reflected in the firm face of Jesus. It was like seeing himself for the very first time. It was like seeing Jesus in a whole new way.

This meal is like that, like a mirror in which we see ourselves, just as we are, with all our imperfections real and imagined, and at the same time just as we were meant to be. This meal is like that, like a painting of Jesus in which we see him more compellingly and ourselves more clearly, precisely because we see us in him and him in us, the way it was meant to be.

So when we take that broken piece of bread today, we will look for the shape of the broken body of Jesus, the crooked, ragged body of Jesus hanging on the cross, and we just might see ourselves, one part of the body partaking of his body. And when we take that cup, we will look for our reflection, for our own eyes—blue, brown, hazel—and we just might see the eyes of Jesus, smarting with sweat, bleary with blood, staring back at us. Us in him; him in us.

God, help us to see in this meal a clearer picture of our Savior and a clearer picture of ourselves, through Jesus, Amen.

And when they had mocked him, they took off the
purple robe and put his own clothes on him.
Then they led him out to crucify him. (Mark 15:20)

The most dramatic moment in human history makes
for odd drama. The hero is center-stage yet silent. His
script is only seven lines long, some whispered, some
groaned through gritted teeth. He gestures simply and
seldom. He is still, pinned as it were to a prop from which
neither the audience nor the other actors can easily
unfasten their eyes. The stage is stark, the scenery sparse,
the props peculiar—hammer, spikes, spear, dice. The
action is minimal at best, at worst awkward. The lighting
is at first too bright, then too night.

Other actors take the stage. Soldiers hammer and
gamble, making light of the weighty moment. Bystanders
assuage their boredom with blasphemy. Priests parrot their
vain victory, ignorant of the irony: "If you come down, we
will believe." Followers weep and wonder, only a few and
from afar. The rest, obvious in their absence, rest off-stage.
Ultimately our eyes are drawn back to the main character,
still still, and we listen to the seven lines and the sudden
silence.

This old drama makes for odd drama. And we find
ourselves left wondering less about the hero than ourselves.

Where will we stand on the stage, with the deriders or the disciples? Will we stand fearfully but faithfully with the women or will we slip off to the wings unable to see or be seen? And what will we say when the next line is ours?

And if we should decide not to try out for this play, not to take part in this odd, old drama, it's too late. By coming to this table we have already accepted a role, we have already joined the cast, we have already taken the stage. This meal to which we are invited reminds us that we are privileged to play a part, a part in the most dramatic moment in human history, in the great drama of redemption.

God, we thank you for Jesus and for his willingness to take the lead, in his name, Amen.

PICTURING THE PAIN

Surely he took up our infirmities and carried our sorrows, yet we considered him stricken by God, smitten by him, and afflicted. (Isaiah 53:4)

Who can forget that print of Jesus kneeling in the garden of Gethsemane? It hung in many a church hall, the first good-morning of a Lord's day, and by many a bed, the last good-night in the lingering light. The eye rises from the massive rock, to the gently clasped hands, to the serenely uplifted face. The soft glow from some supernatural source darts across the nearly-night sky and his face beams back, calm and confident. You can almost hear Jesus say, "Not my will, but thine be done."

But who will picture the pain, the contorted face, the fingers twisted in a tortured knot, the sweat-like drops of blood? Who will paint the "Let this cup pass from me"?

The Lord's Supper is also a popular subject of Christian art. From DaVinci to Dali, Jesus is represented as seated at the table, arms gracefully outstretched. You can almost hear Jesus speaking those words of comfort to his disciples.

But who will picture the pain? Who will paint Jesus "troubled in spirit," saying, "One of you will betray me"? "You will deny me three times"? "You will leave me all alone"?

Even paintings of the Crucifixion often display a face of sweet resignation amidst the thorns and nails. You can almost hear Jesus saying, "Into your hands I commit my spirit."

But we are indebted to those who have shown us the suffering of the "suffering Servant," those who have pictured the pain of "the pain-love of God," those who have not forgotten his "My-God-my-God-why-have-you-forsaken-me" forsakenness.

The Jesus who meets us at this table meets us in the tokens of his suffering—bread like a body broken, the juice of a crushed grape like blood poured out. And the Jesus who meets us here meets us in our own suffering. He not only saves us by his suffering, he suffers with us in our suffering. It is here that we picture the pain.

God, help us sense the pain you felt when you felt our pain. We thank you for Jesus, praying in his name, Amen.

PLAYING "A"

Make every effort to keep the unity of the Spirit through the bond of peace. There is one body and one Spirit—just as you were called to one hope when you were called—one Lord, one faith, one baptism; one God and Father of all, who is over all and through all and in all. (Ephesians 4:3-6)

What is the most important instrument in the orchestra? Is it a string, say a violin, soaring with the sweep of the bow to some tremulous height? Is a wind instrument, like a flute, fluttering its way faster and faster through a trill? Is it a horn, maybe a trombone, mellow and melodious or brassy and brash as the mood dictates? Is it a drum, regulating the rhythm, furnishing the foundation, for the whole orchestra? No, it's none of these.

The most important instrument in the orchestra is the one that makes them one. Before the concert begins, as all the instruments are warming up, playing their own parts, in their own keys, some in tune, some slightly out of tune, the concertmaster nods to the most important instrument in the orchestra—the oboe. And the oboe plays "A." Then each instrument in the orchestra, each with its own distinct sound, tunes itself by playing "A" with the oboe.

Gathering at this table is like playing "A." What we do and say here has the same effect on the body of Christ as the oboe does on the orchestra. It does not demand that we always sound exactly alike. It respects our diversity. And it does not demand that we always play the same note. It respects our harmony. But for one moment it brings us all together, reminding us of the essential oneness we have in Christ.

At this table we play "A," and in so doing "maintain the unity of the Spirit in the bond of peace."

God, our one God, we pray that you bind us together by the one Spirit, born through one baptism into one body with one faith and one hope in our one Lord. Thank you for inviting us to this one table, as different as we are. We pray through Jesus, Amen.

PUBLICANS AND SINNERS

> While Jesus was having dinner at Levi's house, many
> tax collectors and "sinners" were eating with him and
> his disciples, for there were many who followed him.
> When the teachers of the law who were Pharisees saw
> him eating with the "sinners" and tax collectors,
> they asked his disciples: "Why does he eat with tax
> collectors and 'sinners'?" (Mark 2:15,16)

"He eats with publicans and sinners." To the Pharisees
it was an accusation. To think, that the one who claimed to
be the Holy One of God would eat, would share this sacred
moment of human communion, with the un-holiest horde
of humanity! Gentile- and greed-tainted tax collectors,
promiscuous prostitutes, the unclean, the people of the
earth-under-their-fingernails! It has always been true—
He eats with publicans and sinners. But it was never truer
than at the Last Supper.

There was Judas, his white-knuckled money-bag
clutched close to his chest, thirty silver pieces fuller. There
was Peter, good old Get-thee-behind-me, I-never-knew-him,
put-your-sword-away Peter.

There were James and John, hot-tempered as a
summer sons-of-thunderstorm, calling down lightning,
clamoring for the first-shall-be-last best seats. There was
Matthew, a dishonest-to-goodness publican, taxing the

impatience of his patriotic compatriots. There was Simon, the militant, the take-matters-into-his-own-bloody-hands revolutionary.

They were all there, all the disciples, sinners if not publicans, and he ate with them.

It reminds us that, if we ever come to this table *without* recognizing that we are sinners, we are making a grave mistake. For "if we say that we claim to be without sin, we deceive ourselves, and the truth is not in us" (1 John 1:8). But it also reminds us that, if we ever fail to come to this table because we *do* recognize ourselves as sinners, we are making a grave mistake. For "if anybody does sin, we have one who speaks to the Father in our defense, Jesus Christ, the Righteous One, and He is the atoning sacrifice for our sins." (1 John 2:1,2).

Whenever we eat this bread and drink this cup, we celebrate the fact that he still eats, even with us.

God, help us in this meal to see our sin more clearly and our salvation more clearly, because we have seen his sacrifice more clearly, through Jesus, Amen.

Remember Jesus Christ, raised from the dead.
(2 Timothy 2:8)

These are important words, "Remember Jesus Christ, raised from the dead." They are spoken about the foundational fact of the Christian faith. They are spoken to the Christian evangelist Timothy to whom the gospel has been entrusted. And they are spoken by the great apostle Paul on the eve of his death.

These are important words, but they are also somewhat surprising words. Wouldn't Timothy have known all about the resurrection? Wouldn't the disciples Timothy ministered to have understood the meaning of the resurrection? Wasn't it the focus of their faith?

Yes, but Paul knew and Timothy must know and the Christians of Ephesus needed to know, and we had better remember that knowing and remembering are two different things. Of course they knew Jesus Christ, raised from the dead. Now they needed to *remember* Jesus Christ, raised from the dead.

When students get their test papers back and come up to the teacher's desk for a correct answer, their reaction is often, "Oh, I knew that, I just couldn't remember it." That's when teachers have been known to respond, "If you can't remember it, then you didn't really know it." There is a sense in which that is true. But there is a sense in which knowing and remembering are two different things.

The resurrection of Jesus Christ from the dead is the most fundamental fact in all of human history. As Christians, as believers, we know that. But sometimes we don't remember it. Sometimes we don't think resurrection-thoughts. Sometimes we don't maintain resurrection-relationships. Sometimes we don't live resurrection-lives. We need Paul's admonition too. "Remember Jesus Christ, raised from the dead."

But just how do we do that? We remember his resurrection best by remembering his death. That is why we have gathered on Sunday (Resurrection Day) to remember his death, to remember his death until he, the one who could come again only by being raised from the dead, comes again.

God, we thank you for the reality of the resurrection in our lives, and for the way this remembrance of his saving death renews our memory of his victorious resurrection, through Jesus, Amen.

SEEING IS REMEMBERING

No one has ever seen God, but God the One and Only,
who is at the Father's side, has made him known. (John 1:18)

Anyone who has seen me has seen the Father. (John 14:9)

Has it ever happened to you? Someone asks, Do you
remember so-and-so? And you say, I remember the name,
but I can't remember them. They remind you of something
the person did. I remember when that happened, you
respond, but I just can't remember the person. Then
you run into them at the reunion and suddenly, Sure, I
remember you. Seeing is remembering.

Has it ever happened to you? You borrow a book. The
description on the jacket sounds interesting. But it is not
until you get home and start reading it that you realize,
Hey, I've read this before. Seeing is remembering.

Has it ever happened to you? There is this movie that
you know you have seen, but you can't remember a thing
about it, not the actors, the characters, the plot, anything.
Then as you watch it again it all springs back to mind,
the characters, the scenes, maybe even the ending. It's
like seeing something for the first time and remembering
the last time you saw it, all at the same time. Seeing is
remembering.

Has it happened to you? You know you have visited

that site or that city, but you forget what it looked like. You forget, that is, until you return, and suddenly everything seems familiar—the cottages, the lake, the shops. Seeing is remembering.

It happened to the whole human race when Jesus came among us. We had forgotten the God who had created us and cared for us. But then Jesus came and when we saw him, we knew God again. Seeing was remembering.

In fact it happens to us every Sunday, when we see that fragment of bread, when we see the fruit of the vine. It happens to us every Sunday, because as important as the words are—This is my body, This cup is the new covenant in my blood—the objects we hold, the elements in our eyes are also important. Seeing is remembering.

God, help us to see you in him, through Jesus, Amen.

STAY WITH US

Now that same day two of them were going to a village
called Emmaus, about seven miles from Jerusalem.
They were talking with each other about everything that
had happened. As they talked and discussed these things
with each other, Jesus himself came up and walked along
with them; but they were kept from recognizing him.
As they approached the village to which they were going,
Jesus acted as if he were going farther. But they urged
him strongly, "Stay with us, for it is nearly evening;
the day is almost over." So he went in to stay with them.
(Luke 24:13-16, 28,29)

They hadn't recognized him, as he joined the river of
returnees flowing toward Emmaus, Passover past. They
could easily have ignored his prying questions. And they
still hadn't recognized him, when he sculpted the scriptures
anew for them. They could easily have avoided his
inspiring instruction.

But there was something about him that made them
say, say to this strangely familiar stranger, even insist,
"Stay with us." And when he did, he became known to
them in the breaking of the bread.

The risen Lord can be ignored, as he was by the other
casual travelers who saw him on the road to Emmaus that
day, saw him as just another accidental tourist.

And the risen Lord can be a source of temporary inspiration during a brief discouragement or disappointment, one to be let go of, with all but our eyes, which wistfully watch him walking wistfully away, receding in the dust and dusk of the evening of our minds.

Or the risen Lord can be apprehended, even before we comprehend the full import of his identity, persuaded that we must persist in his presence, living in the lively hope that he will be known to us in the breaking of the bread.

And so we say today, we insist, "Stay with us."

And he says, "This is my body broken for you. This cup is the new covenant in my blood, poured out for you." Which is another way of saying, "I will."

God, we pray that you stay with us, and open our eyes, so that we can sense what we cannot see, through Jesus, Amen.

THE BEAUTY OF GOLGOTHA

Carrying his own cross, he went out to the place of
the Skull (which in Aramaic is called Golgotha).
Here they crucified him, and with him two others—
one on each side and Jesus in the middle. (John 19:17, 18)

Sometimes some of the most horrible things happen in
some of the most beautiful places.

Think of the mystery and beauty of the South American
rain forest, the surfeit of too-green-to-be-true foliage,
flowers blooming like freeze-frame fireworks, birds pluming
in a dash-splash of color. Then watch the clear-cutters
turn that paradise of feather and frond into a bare, brown
graveyard.

Think of the white-washed buildings, white as a
cloud in a clear sky, and the sea, pale as emerald, clear
as crystal, and the towering green cedars on the towering
white mountains of Lebanon. Then watch the mortars
crack the mortar and crush the homes, the sea fume and
foam with smoky-black refuse, the mountains moan and
mourn under the bombs.

Think of the rock and rolling meadows and pasture
plots, the quiet patchwork quilt stitched by farm hands,
under the creased brows of the heads and the hills around
Gettysburg. Then watch the cannons bawling, and the

plotted Pickett fences shattered like the door board of the sewing woman so dead.

Sometimes some of the most horrible things—like death and destruction— happen in some of the most beautiful places.

Golgotha, on the other hand, may have been a singularly horrible place—a bare and barren rock to begin with, now stamped and stippled by the studded sandals of the soldiers, scarred and scored by the dug-drug crosses, empty poles and holes, like the sockets of a skull. The Place of the Skull would have been one of the most horrible places in the world.

But sometimes some of the most beautiful things happen in some of the most horrible places. Like the death, the sacrificial death of our loving Lord, breathing out mercy in the midst of our meanness and madness. May this meal remind us of the beautifully horrible thing that happened in that horribly beautiful place.

God, grace our lives, however horrible our circumstances, with the beauty of your grace, through Jesus, Amen.

So he got up from the meal, took off his outer clothing,
and wrapped a towel around his waist. After that,
he poured water into a basin and began to wash
his disciples' feet, drying them with the towel that
was wrapped around him. (John 13:4,5)

There's a mystery in the Gospel of John. It's in chapter
thirteen. It's the mystery of the missing meal. There's a
meal going on all right, the same upper-room supper we
read about elsewhere, but *the* meal is missing. There is
not one word about the broken bread or the covenant cup,
no this-is-my-body, no this-is-the-cup. It's the case of the
missing meal.

But there are clues, tell-tale marks of the meal
all around the room, footprints and fingerprints and
voiceprints that give evidence, incontrovertible evidence,
beyond-a-shadow-of-a-doubt evidence, that the Lord's
Supper is hidden there somewhere in the Last Supper.

There is the clue of the footwashing—your basic basin,
with towel, and the words, "If then I have washed your feet,
you also ought to wash one another's feet."

Clue number two? Jesus' response to Peter's brash
brush-off: "If I don't wash your feet, you have no part in
me."

Then there is the third clue, their consternation at "Where I am going you cannot follow now," followed by their relief at "but you shall follow afterward."

And finally, like the echo of a whisper, clue four: "By this shall all people know that you are my disciples, if you have love for one another."

There they are: clue one, sacrificial service; clue two, participation in Christ; clue three, anticipation of future life in his presence; and clue four, shared love, shared life.

It's right there after all, right there where it isn't, in John 13. The case of the missing meal is solved whenever we gather around this table, solved by our own commitment to sacrificial service, by our participation in Christ's death, by our hopeful anticipation of his return, and by our love for one another.

God, help us see the significance of this meal everywhere we look, and help us see your Son every time we meet at this meal, through Jesus, Amen.

THE COMPANY OF TRAITORS

While they were reclining at the table eating, he said,
"I tell you the truth, one of you will betray me—one who
is eating with me." They were saddened, and one by one
they said to him, "Surely not I?" (Mark 14:18,19)

When Jesus ate his Last Supper, he placed himself in
the company of traitors. He chose to eat at last with those
who would disappoint him the most. One would betray
him. One would repeatedly deny him. All would flee in fear.
Later they would continue to confuse his kingdom with
theirs.

Jesus sat in the company of traitors. But what is really
striking is not that he sat with them, but what he did for
them. He washed the feet that would run—not—walk to
betray him. He promised his presence to the ones who
would abandon him. He prayed unity for those who would
scatter. He invited the one who would dishonor him to take
the seat of honor. He died for the very ones who denied and
deserted and disappointed him.

We too sit around this table in the company of traitors,
as the company of traitors. We eat with preachers who
provoke us, with elders who may be in error, with teachers
tempted to twist the truth, with janitors and youth workers
and secretaries whose work we would do differently (if we
would!). We sit with spouses who are distant, sup with

children who are disobedient. We pass the plate to people who let us down or embarrass us or irritate us. And we feed ourselves.

But when we do, sit in this company of traitors, we enact one of the wonders of this wonderful meal. We remind ourselves that Jesus came to wash dirty feet, to serve, to forgive, to die for these very, very disappointing people. We remind ourselves that this company of traitors with whom we gather is also the company of the redeemed. We remind ourselves that to be among the company of the forgiven is to be a part of the company of forgivers.

God, forgive us for forgetting that you have forgiven us, traitors that we are, and for forgetting to forgive our fellow traitors, through Jesus, Amen.

THE MEDICINE OF IMMORTALITY

A man ought to examine himself before he eats of
the bread and drinks of the cup. (1 Corinthians 11:28)

Have you ever been sick, so sick you went to the doctor,
so sick she gave you one of those knock-it-out-of-you-once-
and-for-all shots or some of those knock-you-out pills?

And while you lay there awkwardly on the examining
table, did she try to explain to you what the drugs were and
how they would work in your body?

And did you lie there thinking that you weren't really
in the mood for listening to all this, or that even if you were
you couldn't have conjured up enough high school biology
to understand her explanation, or that even if you could
understand what she was saying the medicine would have
its same wonderfully healing effects?

You may not have understood completely or at all what
the medicine would do for you, but you were certainly
better for having taken it.

Now we come to the Lord's table, which is, according
to Paul, a kind of "examining" table. We come now to eat
the Lord's Supper, which some of the earliest Christians
were fond of calling "the medicine of immortality." It's an
interesting phrase. It implies an illness, and a cure. It
implies that the meal can somehow heal.

Ever since those early days Christians have been trying to explain just what this meal is and how it works. And in the midst of our sometimes spiritual sicknesses and fevered states we have tried to listen to their explanations—transubstantiation, consubstantiation, real presence, symbolic presence, mystical presence.

Many of us have never heard those terms, and most of us don't understand them even if we've heard them. But we wonder if, even if we understood this meal better, it would "work" any better. Or to put it another way, we are confident that "the medicine of immortality" will still have its same wonderfully healing effects.

We may not understand it completely when we eat the bread and drink the cup, but we are certainly better for having eaten.

God, we thank you for the honest diagnosis of our sin, and for the prescription of salvation though your Son, in his name, Amen.

THE RENDING OF HEAVEN

As soon as Jesus was baptized, he went up out of
the water. At that moment heaven was opened,
and he saw the Spirit of God descending
like a dove and lighting on him. (Matthew 3:16)

And when Jesus had cried out again in a loud voice,
he gave up his spirit. At that moment the curtain of the
temple was torn in two from top to bottom. (Matthew 27:50,51)

As Jesus was coming up out of the water, the dark and
formless deep over which God's Spirit had once hovered,
the heavens themselves were torn open. We call it the
baptism, but it was the rending of Heaven. The physical
barrier between Our-Father-who-art-in-Heaven and all
on-earth-as-it-is-in-Heaven humanity was torn apart. The
Son of God was revealed to the children of God as the Son
of God.

And with a loud cry, a cry that shook the foundations of
the well-founded earth, the curtain of the temple, the sky-
blue curtain stitched like the night sky with embroidered
silver stars, the curtain that separated the heavenly, the
Holy of Holies, from the earthly, was torn in two, from its
heavenward top to its brush-the-earth bottom. We call
it the crucifixion, but it was the rending of Heaven. The
ritual barrier between the Holy One and unholy humanity,
between the mercy seat of God and merciless humanity,

was torn apart. The Son of God was reconciling the children of God to God.

In between those two great rendings, those rendings of Heaven, in between the voice that said, This is my beloved son in whom I am well-pleased, and the voice that said, Father, into your hands I commit my spirit, Jesus took bread and broke it. There was no sky-diving dove, no earth-shaking earthquake, just the ripping of the unleavened loaf. We call it the Last Supper, but it was the rending of Heaven. The last barrier, the barrier of forgetfulness, between our "Where-are-you?" God and us hiding-in-the-garden humanity, was torn apart. The children of God were remembering God through the Son of God.

Do this in remembrance of him.

God, help us to remember your presence, your Heaven-rending, veil-rending, heart-rending presence, through Jesus, Amen.

THE SHADOW OF DEATH

Now that same day two of them were going to a village called Emmaus, about seven miles from Jerusalem. They were talking with each other about everything that had happened. As they talked and discussed these things with each other, Jesus himself came up and walked along with them, but they were kept from recognizing him. (Luke 24:13-16)

It was resurrection day, but they were headed home. It was resurrection day, but the Passover was past, over, and they were going home. It was resurrection day, but they were still hung over from the soberness of it all, with the three-day-darker darkness of the crucifixion looming on their horizon, filling their eyes. It was resurrection day, but all they could talk about were the last events of the last few days, stringing and restringing them like dusky pearls that wouldn't hang together, remembering, rehearsing, reciting, repeating them, as if one more time through and it might all turn out differently, it might all make some sense.

But then they were joined by Jesus. What-in-the-world-was-he-doing-there Jesus caught up with them, fell in with the crest-fallen pair. But they didn't recognize him.

Was it too dim in the fading light? Was it some supernatural stupor? Had they not known Jesus well? Had he changed? Were they tired, preoccupied? Was the darkness of his death too deep to allow them to see the light of his life?

Was it that they, like the apostles before them, were simply unable or unwilling to process the paradox, the paradox of a suffering Messiah, a crucified Lord? Had they been so unwilling to accept the fact that the one they had lived with could die that they were unable to accept the fact that the one who had died could be alive? Were they so overwhelmed with the impossibility of his death that they could not even consider the possibility of his life?

Is that why they could only, finally recognize the risen Lord, realize the reality of the resurrection, in the breaking of the bread, in the tokens of his death?

And can we?

God, may these shadows of his death be for us the evidences of his life, and ours, through Jesus, Amen.

THIS MEAL, EVERY MEAL

Taking the five loaves and two fish and looking up
to heaven, he gave thanks and broke the loaves. Then he
gave them to his disciples to set before the people. He also
divided the two fish among them all. They all ate and were
satisfied, and the disciples picked up twelve basketfuls
of broken pieces of bread and fish. The number of the men
who had eaten was five thousand. (Mark 6:41-44)

When he had taken the seven loaves and given thanks,
he broke them and gave them to his disciples to set
before the people, and they did so. They had a few small
fish as well; he gave thanks for them also and told the
disciples to distribute them. The people ate and were
satisfied. Afterward the disciples picked up seven
basketfuls of broken pieces that were left over.
About four thousand men were present. (Mark 8:6-9)

While they were eating, Jesus took bread, gave thanks,
and broke it, and gave it to his disciples, saying,
"Take it; this is my body." Then he took the cup, gave
thanks and offered it to them, and they all drank from it.
"This is my blood of the covenant, which is poured out
for many," he said to them. (Mark 14:22-24)

There is a sense in which every meal—the feeding
of the five thousand, the feeding of the four thousand,
the Last Supper, last night's supper—has been a

foreshadowing of this meal, memorializing the gift of life in Jesus' death. The recognition of the gift of God's grace in this meal reminds us that in every meal, mundane or miraculous, we must recognize the gracious gifts of God.

And there is a sense in which this meal, this Lordly Supper, both mundane and miraculous, sanctifies every meal, making each one a celebration of life through this death. The regular recognition of God's gifts for which we express thanks in the name of Jesus each time we eat reminds us of the inexpressible gift—Jesus himself—which we recognize at this table.

God, there is no question that we will take and break, eat and drink; we ask only to remember Jesus whenever we do, in his name, Amen.

Because there is one loaf, we, who are many, are one body,
for we all partake of the one loaf. (1 Corinthians 10:17)

So then, my brothers, when you come together to eat,
wait for each other. (1 Corinthians 11:33)

The fourth day of every July reminds us that the
United States of America was founded on the principle
of independence. But the first day of every week of every
month reminds us that the Church of the Lord Jesus Christ
was founded on the principle of interdependence.

The document on which our country was founded, *The
Declaration of Independence*, makes that principle very
clear, in its title and in its content: "We hold these truths
to be self-evident, that all men are created equal; that they
are endowed by their Creator with certain unalienable
rights; that among these are life, liberty, and the pursuit of
happiness."

But the document on which our church was founded,
the New Testament, might well be called "The Declaration
of Interdependence," a principle its title and its contents
make very clear. In fact we might sum up one of its great
themes by saying, "We hold these truths to be evident
in the revelation of Jesus Christ, that all Christians are
created in community; that they are endowed by their

Creator with certain unalienable responsibilities; that among these are shared life, mutual service, and the pursuit of one another's holiness."

So just as surely as red-white-and-blue bunting, and seventy-six-trombones-led-the-big parade parades, and star-spangled banners are signs of our country's longing for independence, this gathering, our sing-them-over-again-to-each-other songs, our overheard prayers, our mutual exhortations, are all signs of our congregation's longing for interdependence.

And if we listen to Paul—"Because there is one loaf, we, who are many, are one body" and "When you come together to eat, wait for one another"—we will realize that this meal, this shared meal, especially this meal, is our loud-as-a-firecracker-on-the-Fourth-of-July Declaration of Interdependence.

God, we pray that our Communion here today might help us focus not only on the body of the Christ but also on the community of Christ, through Jesus, Amen.

WHAT'S-HIS-NAME?

Now that same day two of them were going to a village
called Emmaus, about seven miles from Jerusalem. . . .
When he was at the table with them, he took bread, gave
thanks, broke it, and began to give it to them.
Then their eyes were opened and they recognized him.

(Luke 24:13,30,31)

How strange of Luke to leave out one of the names—
Luke, the gospel writer who above all the others wanted to
get the just-the-facts-ma'am facts, good old who-was-the-
emperor, who-was-the-governor, who-was-the-king, and
what-were-their names Luke. He names Zechariah and
Elizabeth, Simeon and Anna, Lazarus the beggar, even
Zacchaeus the publican. But oddly enough he names only
one of the two on the road to Emmaus—there was Cleopas
and then there was . . . what's-his-name?

But on the other hand how absolutely predictable of
Luke to be the only gospel writer to highlight this story
of the risen Lord, appearing to two such unknown almost
anonymous travelers to Emmaus. We have no idea who
they were, what the name of one of them was, what they
knew, thought, or believed about Jesus, where the road to
Emmaus was, even where Emmaus was, for that matter.

For Luke, telling the story of these unknowns who
recognized the risen Jesus in the breaking of the bread was

just the point. It's like being the only gospel writer to tell about the angels telling about the birth of Jesus to those unknown, unnamed shepherds. It was precisely the point.

The Messiah came for us, the Son of God died for us, the crucified Christ rose for us, all us nameless, faceless people. Jesus came and died and rose for the what's-his-names of the world, so that the simplest of people, unnamed and unknown, might hear his name and know him, recognize him in the simplest of actions, in the breaking of the bread.

This is his body broken for us, us what's-his-names. This is the cup of the new covenant in his blood, poured out for us what's-his-names. Let us recognize the risen Lord in the breaking of the bread.

God, thank you for giving him the name that is above every name, so that every anonymous knee, including our own, might bow before him, in his name, Amen.

When he noticed how the guests picked the places
of honor at the table, he told them this parable:
"When someone invites you to a wedding feast,
do not take the place of honor. For everyone who
exalts himself will be humbled, and he who
humbles himself will be exalted." (Luke 14:7, 11)

If Christ came to Communion, where would he sit?
Would he first find the front, so the First-born, the First-
fruits, would be the first served? Or would he first find the
foot and the feet?

If Christ came to Communion, what would he do?
Would he preside, striding to the front uninvited yet
unrestrained, or rising only at someone's insistence, to
instruct us on the depth of his death, on the mystery of the
meal?

If Christ came to Communion, what would he do?
Would he serve at the table, patiently, purposefully passing
the Body of Christ, being the Body of Christ, bearing the
Body of Christ to the Body of Christ?

If Christ came to Communion, what would he do?
Would he have prepared the meal, baked the bread,
without rising (until later, that is), pouring out the fruit of
the vine, filling each cup with care?

Would he, as it were, clean up, wiping away the leftovers of the merely miraculous meal, rinsing the remnant of wine out of each cup, rubbing off the red crescent sticking to the lip?

Or would he have been the one who'd winnowed the wheat, ground the grain, gathered the grapes—the Sower whose plowing and planting and plucking we take so for granted as we dig in?

If Christ came to Communion, what would he be—guest, host, servant? And what would he do—prepare, preside, pass out, clean up?

Wouldn't he at least be what he was at last—the host? Not the host at the head of the table, but the host here on the table—a Body broken, Christ crushed.

God, help us to take seriously being served this day, as if by the one who came not to be served, and help us to take seriously serving every day, as if in the name of the one who came to serve, through Jesus, Amen.

YOU . . . WITH ME

One of the criminals who hung there hurled insults
at him: "Aren't you the Christ? Save yourself and us!"
But the other criminal rebuked him. "Don't you fear God,"
he said, "since you are under the same sentence? . . .
Then he said, "Jesus, remember me when you come into
your kingdom." Jesus answered him, "I tell you the truth,
today you will be with me in paradise." (Luke 23:39-43)

Today you will be with me in paradise. According to
some, the most important word in this wonderful promise
is "Today." But they argue over what it means. Do believers
go to Heaven immediately at death, or someday?

Others say "paradise" is the key word. But they debate
whether it refers to Heaven or a region of Heaven. They
wonder if everyone goes there, or just some, and who. If
they go there forever, or a time, and how long.

"Will be" has attracted some attention. Does the future
tense imply the immediate future, the split-second after
death claimed the criminal, or the far-distant future, a
general resurrection at Jesus' return?

But the most important words in this promise are
"you . . . with me." Today *you* will be *with me* in Paradise.
Jesus was speaking personally and interpersonally, not
chronologically or geographically. To Jesus the thief was
a person in need, in need of hope. To the thief Jesus was

the person who would establish his kingdom in spite of his death, because of his death. "Remember *me* when *you* come into *your* kingdom."

It reminds us of two other parallel promises. "And if I go and prepare a place for you, I will come back and take *you* to be *with me*." "And surely *I* will be *with you* always, to the very end of the age." You . . . with me—about that there is no debate. On the cross he gave the promise to a criminal. At this table he does the same for us.

God, we thank you for being with us now at this table, this table which is a token of the promise that we will always be with you, through Jesus, Amen.

SCRIPTURAL INDEX

TOPICAL INDEX